PILIPINTO

PILIPINTO

The Jungle Adventures
of a Missionary's Daughter

Valerie Elliot Shepard

P&R
PUBLISHING
P.O.BOX 817 • PHILLIPSBURG • NEW JERSEY 08865-0817

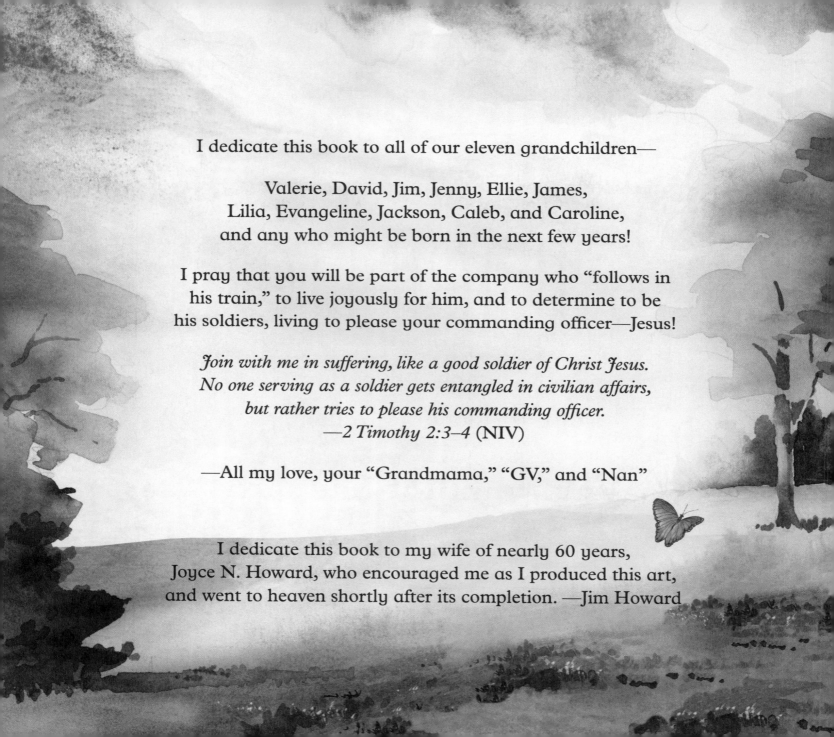

I dedicate this book to all of our eleven grandchildren—

Valerie, David, Jim, Jenny, Ellie, James,
Lilia, Evangeline, Jackson, Caleb, and Caroline,
and any who might be born in the next few years!

I pray that you will be part of the company who "follows in
his train," to live joyously for him, and to determine to be
his soldiers, living to please your commanding officer—Jesus!

Join with me in suffering, like a good soldier of Christ Jesus.
No one serving as a soldier gets entangled in civilian affairs,
but rather tries to please his commanding officer.
—2 Timothy 2:3–4 (NIV)

—All my love, your "Grandmama," "GV," and "Nan"

I dedicate this book to my wife of nearly 60 years,
Joyce N. Howard, who encouraged me as I produced this art,
and went to heaven shortly after its completion. —Jim Howard

Table of Contents

Chapter 1

A Home in the Jungle

Valerie's eyes widen in wonder as the parasol ants march one by one across the soggy trail. Each carries a piece of a leaf over its head, sheltering it from raindrops. The long line of these tiny creatures seems endless. These clever ants remind her how happy she is to live in the Amazon rainforest of Ecuador.

In the rainforest there are many wild animals that hunt and play. Valerie hears monkeys chattering in the trees. She sees colorful birds flying overhead their bright feathers flashing. She wonders why the parasol ants work so hard, while the sloths are content to sleep all day in the trees.

Many people make their home in the Amazon rainforest. Valerie calls them Indians. The Indians live in groups called tribes. The jungle has been their home for a long time. They work hard with their hands making thatched roofs for their huts, and they hunt in the forest for food. There are no cars, buses, or planes, no grocery stores, or shopping malls.

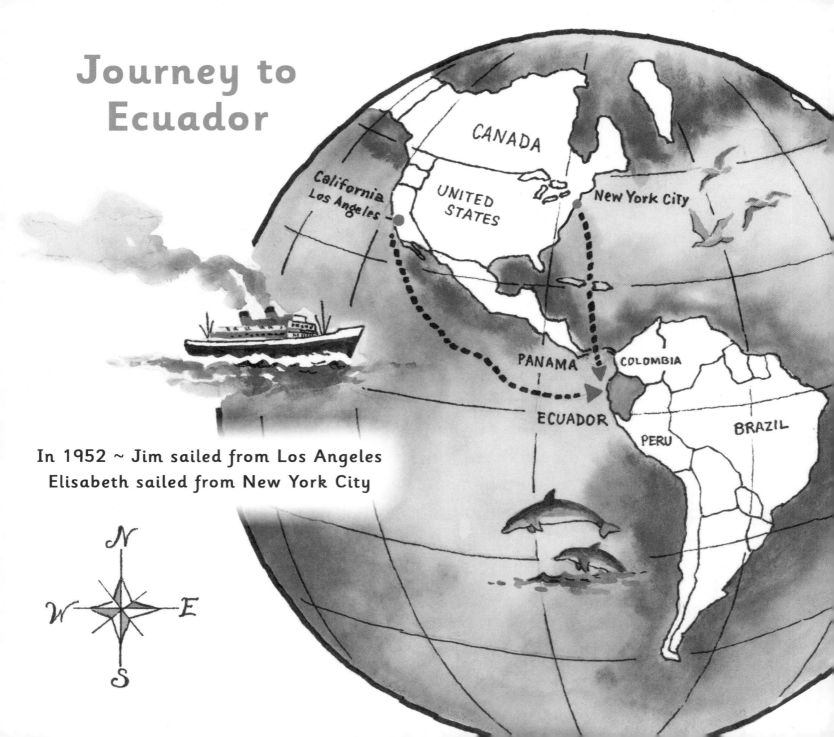

Journey to Ecuador

In 1952 ~ Jim sailed from Los Angeles
Elisabeth sailed from New York City

Valerie was born in Ecuador, but her parents, Jim Elliot, and Elisabeth Howard, grew up in the United States. When her parents were young students, they went to school at Wheaton College in Illinois. In 1947 they met and became friends. Jim and Elisabeth both loved God. They wanted to serve him by telling people who had never heard about Jesus the gospel story. Do you know what "the gospel" is? It's the true and wonderful story, the "good news" of how God loved the world. He sent his only Son, Jesus, to live and die for lost sinners so that those who believe in him will be saved from their sins and go to heaven when they die.

One day a Dr. Tidmarsh came to bring Jim some important news: "Hey Jim, I want to tell you about an Indian tribe in Ecuador. They are hard to find because they are not friendly to outsiders. So far, no one has been able to tell them that Jesus loves them!" This news lit a flame in Jim's heart. He prayed, "O Lord, send me to this tribe!"

It would not be easy to find these Indians. First Jim and Elisabeth traveled by boat to Ecuador. They sailed on freighters for three weeks until they reached the port city of Guayaquil. From there they flew to Quito, the capital city of Ecuador. In Quito they learned Spanish, the main language spoken in Ecuador.

After they left Quito, Elisabeth went west of the Andes mountains toward the coast. Jim went east of the Andes to a little village called Shandia.

Jim invited his friend Pete Fleming to come along. Together they worked with the Quichua Indians who lived there. The Indians were friendly and were glad that Jim and Pete cared about them. Shandia was a perfect place to build a mission station. The Quichuas had already built an airstrip so airplanes could bring in supplies. The Indian men and boys took care of the airstrip by cutting back the jungle overgrowth every day. They even helped Jim and Pete clear more land. Together, they built a chapel and a school for boys.

Soon, Elisabeth moved closer to Shandia. Jim was very happy that he could see her. Still, they had to walk all day to meet each other! They talked about how they wanted to spend their life together, teaching the jungle Indians about Jesus. Jim told Elisabeth, "You must learn to speak Quichua before we get married. Then we can both make friends with the Indians. We will live at Shandia, and I will build a good house for you."

On October 8, 1953, Jim and Elisabeth got married! Just as Jim promised, he found a beautiful spot for the house. It was near the Atun Yacu River where you could see the Andes mountains. Building the house was hard work! Jim's father came all the way from the United States to help him.

Jim made the house out of concrete so it would be very strong. It had a metal roof and screen windows. He put a barrel on the roof to catch the rain—now the house had running water! He even installed electricity. It was a most unusual and wonderful house in the middle of the jungle!

Soon Elisabeth and Jim were expecting a baby! Their friend, Nate Saint, was a pilot. He flew them to Shell Mera where Elisabeth was going to have her baby at Nate and Marge Saint's home.

On February 27, 1955, Valerie was born. She was her parents' first and only child. Elisabeth and Jim were happy to have a baby girl! They flew back to Shandia to take her home. Many Quichuas gathered at the airstrip to welcome them.

The Quichuas and the Elliots were good friends. The men eagerly came to Jim's Bible class, and the boys attended school. Because Jim shared the good news of Jesus with them, many in Shandia learned to love Jesus too!

But Jim kept praying for the tribe that Dr. Tidmarsh had told him about—the tribe that did not want to make friends with outsiders. They called themselves Waorani (Wao for short). That means "the people."

March 6, 1955

One week ago today, Valerie arrived. Dr. Fuller delivered her here in the Saints' house, with Liz, his wife, in attendance. Jim was with me every minute, which meant more to me than he will ever know. . . . What a joy to hear her first cry, and to see our own daughter!

O, Lord—We give her back to Thee, in gratitude, and ask Thy holy wisdom and love in guiding and caring for her.

Chapter 2

Meeting the Waorani

One afternoon, a neighbor came to tell Jim that a member of their tribe had been killed by the Waorani. This was the same tribe that Jim had been praying for! Although the news was sad, it lit a fire of hope in Jim's heart. Right away he shared his excitement with Elisabeth: "If we can find them, we can tell them the gospel story!"

Jim's four missionary friends—Nate Saint, Ed McCully, Roger Youdarian, and Pete Fleming—were also praying for the Waorani. They wanted to tell them the good news about Jesus, but they knew it would be dangerous. The Quichuas called the Wao "savages" because the Wao were not friendly. They killed people with spears and everyone was afraid of their angry ways.

Jim's friend Nate was a pilot for the Missionary Aviation Fellowship. It was his job to fly a small airplane to all the missionary outposts. He delivered food, medicine, and mail. Nate began looking for the Waorani as he flew above the treetops in his airplane. His search took a long time because the Waorani were nomadic. That means they moved their huts to new places so they could find more food to eat.

Finally, Nate found a cluster of Waorani huts. He decided to take each of his missionary friends along with him in the airplane. They planned to bring gifts to the Waorani once a week by lowering a bucket from the plane to give them matches, knives, ax heads, and cooking pots! They  decided to shout through a megaphone from the airplane, yelling phrases Jim had learned: "We are your friends! We want to see you!"

For many weeks the men flew over the Wao huts, sending down gifts. In return, the Wao began to put gifts of their own into the bucket. They gave a crown made from macaw feathers, a comb, smoked fish, and a roasted monkey's paw. (They ate monkeys, so they thought the missionaries would like it!)

Valerie was a ten month old baby, just learning to crawl, when her father and his four friends decided to meet the Waorani. The men flew onto a sandy beach near the Wao settlement. They built a treehouse to stay in. They hoped the Waorani would come to visit them.

A few days later, two women and one man came out of the jungle to say hello. The Wao were friendly, curious, and very talkative. The Indians did not understand anything the missionaries said but chattered away as if the white men could understand them. When they said goodbye that night, it seemed like the Wao were happy to be their friends!

Soon, as Nate flew over the Wao settlement, he hoped that his new friends would come out to wave at him. But no one did. He radioed his wife, Marge: "Maybe the Waorani are coming to meet us on the beach! Pray for an afternoon service!" That night on January 8, 1956, Marge and Elisabeth and the other missionary wives waited by the radio to hear from Nate. But no news came—so they prayed and they waited.

Three days later, the Ecuadorian Army and the American military sent out helicopters, and a search party went out to find the five missionaries. They trekked through the jungle for three days. They found four of their friends' bodies in the river by the treehouse. Later, they found the body of the fifth man downriver. The Waorani had killed them with spears. These five friends had given their lives, hoping to share the love and good news of Jesus. The sad news was reported around the world. Everyone prayed for their families.

Elisabeth and little Valerie stayed in Shandia with the Quichua Indians. Elisabeth and the other wives prayed for the Waorani tribe—that someday they would hear the good news about Jesus . . .

Sept. 1961

Waking up one morning she said to me,

"When are we going?"

"Where?" I asked.

"Up where God lives."

Oct. 1961

"Will we go through a rainbow when we go to God's house?"

Chapter 3

A Surprising Invitation

A few years later, when Valerie is almost three years old, two Waorani women, Mintaka and Mankamu, come out of the jungle to talk with the Quichuas. They are afraid of their families' angry ways and want to live with the peaceful Quichua Indians instead. The Quichuas are surprised and don't know what to think of the two women who want to stay with them.

When Elisabeth hears about these visitors, she quickly goes to meet them. The women are pleasant and friendly, so she takes Valerie to meet them too. Mintaka and Mankamu talk constantly. After a few weeks, Elisabeth invites them into her home. Now she can hear their language every day. She begins writing down the sounds they make for the very first time.

Mintaka likes to call Elisabeth *Gikari*. (*Gikari* means "woodpecker." They choose this name because of her pointed nose!) They love Gikari because she teaches them God's words. Mankamu tells Gikari that she wants to teach her own children to live differently. The Waorani people know it is wrong to kill others, but they have made excuses to kill outsiders and anyone who makes them angry.

Now after learning God's ways, Mankamu believes that God wants her people to stop killing. She and Mintaka ask Gikari for help. They talk excitedly to Valerie and her mama: "You will go with us, Gikari. We know the trail. We will carry Valerie. We will live with Gikita, my husband. He will fish for us and bring us meat from the forest."

"We will have a good house," the women tell Gikari. "There will be plenty of plantain and manioc to eat. The plane can drop your food for you, and we will help you pick it up. You will see our children. They will love you and your child. You will take your needle and help the sick people. We will all live well."

Gikari asks, "But won't they spear us?"

"It is the downriver ones who spear," the women reply. "They are far away." "But your people speared my husband," Gikari says. "They will spear me." "Gikari!" Mankamu cries. "Your husband was a man! You are a woman! We will say, 'She is good. She is like our mother. We love her.'"

Mankamu tells Gikari, "When I get home, I'll say to my brother, 'God's Word says don't be afraid, don't kill, and don't lie. You must tell the others this. Then we will live well. Just think about hunting for our food; don't think about killing people. As time goes by, you'll get to know Gikari. Don't be afraid of her. Build a house for her and another house where her friends can come to sleep. She will teach you God's words. You must listen and teach the children too. Listen well— hear them sing. It is good, what they teach.'" Mankamu smiles broadly, her eyes bright. She is hoping for a new life for her people!

Gikari is hopeful too. Still, in the early morning hours she lies awake. She wonders if she can believe the words of a Waorani woman. She asks the Lord for his word.

Then she remembers God's words from the book of Nehemiah Chapter 9. Nehemiah reminds her of God's promises and how he took care of his people in the desert:

"You are the Lord, the God who chose Abram and brought him out of Ur of the Chaldeans and gave him the name Abraham. You found his heart faithful before you, and made with him the covenant to give to his offspring the land. . . . And you have kept your promise, for you are righteous. . . . By a pillar of cloud, you led them in the day, and by a pillar of fire in the night to light for them the way in which they should go. . . . You gave your good Spirit to instruct them. . . . You sustained them in the wilderness, and they lacked nothing. . . . You brought them into the land. . . . And you subdued before them the inhabitants of the land."

These words from the Bible give Elisabeth courage. There is hard work ahead! But she thanks God that he is going to take her and little Valerie to the Waorani tribe with Mintaka and Mankamu.

Chapter 4

Jungle Trek

In the morning, the Quichua Indians watch in surprise as Gikari collects the items she thinks they'll need for their trip to Tiwaenu where the Waorani live. Gikari packs two pots, two plates, clothing, a tape recorder, blankets, some books, and a Bible. Meanwhile, Valerie plays with her friends and chases small animals outside. The Quichuas call her Pilipinto, which means "butterfly," because she is always eager to play. They will miss Gikari and her little Pilipinto.

The Waorani have been told that Gikari, "the very tall lady with jaguar eyes," is coming to live with them. Some Waorani and a few Quichua Indians lead the way to Tiwaenu.

A very kind man, Fermin, carries Pilipinto in a wooden chair he has built and strapped to his back! From her safe perch, Pilipinto watches the ground going backward and the other Indians walking in single file behind them.

It rains every day in the Amazon, so the trail is muddy, and slippery. The forest is thick with vines and branches. The tall trees have leaves in all shapes and sizes. The light is dim and cool, but sometimes a bright sunbeam finds its way to the jungle floor. They walk quickly but quietly, careful not to disturb the poisonous snakes lying on the trail or hanging down from the vines. They know that if they disturb them, the snakes will strike!

Snakes do not scare the Quichuas as much as the Waorani do. "Angry Waorani may be hiding behind the trees, watching us!" the Quichuas say. "They might jump out and kill us!"

But Gikari trusts in God. She keeps telling them, "God will take care of us. Do not be afraid."

The air is filled with damp, earthy smells and the sweet pungent odor of tropical flowers and fruits. Pilipinto loves these smells. She especially loves hearing the gentle pat, pat, pat of raindrops dripping from the leaves. She observes tiny brilliant-colored birds sipping the droplets. She sees bright green tree frogs sitting peacefully on leaves. Sometimes cold drops of water land on her head, but she is used to it. Parasol ants don't have that problem!

They stay dry under the bits of leaves they carry over their heads. They are bringing the leaves home to build their nests.

It will take three more days to get to Tiwaenu. Most of the time Pilipinto walks. When she is tired she rides in the wooden chair. Sometimes she falls asleep, and then her head rolls back and forth as they turn curves in the trail.

One night in the pouring rain they take shelter on an island. Pilipinto crawls into the warm woolen sleeping bag that her mama made for her. During the night, Gikari wakes her. "Quick!" The Indians are hurrying to gather their belongings. The island is flooding! Jumping into a canoe, they paddle to a high bank above the rising river. Here they can sleep safely for the rest of the night.

How can the Indians find a dry spot on the bank in the darkness? God is taking care of them!

In the early morning light, Gikari shows Pilipinto some turtle tracks that come straight up from the river. They follow the tracks and find a well-covered hole where a turtle laid her eggs in the sand. The Indians cook the eggs in the hot ashes of their fire. They look like rubbery ping-pong balls. The yolks have a grainy texture, but they are delicious! Pilipinto eats them hungrily. Thank you, God! Breakfast is served!

Chapter 5

Tiwaenu

Fermin walks faster as he senses a clearing in the jungle up ahead. He yells back to them, "Shami, shami!" which means "Come, come!" Finally, after a long three-day hike, they have reached Tiwaenu!

At this camp, the Waorani have cut down trees to build their huts. They use their feet to stomp the earth flat to make floors. There are always six poles set in place to hold up each thatched roof. There are no walls. Hammocks hang between the poles, and a fire burns in the center. The fires burn for cooking by day and for warmth at night.

The Waorani build a new hut for Gikari and her daughter. Its thatched roof comes down almost to the ground to keep the wind and rain out. The Indians dig a ditch for them underneath the overhang to collect rainwater.

A rainy night ~ I in the hammock by the gasoline lamp, Val in her small bed beside me. "Mama, when you put your hand like this you can hear the ocean!" (cupping her hand over her ear) "Try it."

Pilipinto needs a bed to sleep on, so Waorani men cut bamboo branches and tie them to a platform of logs. Now she can sleep next to her mama's hammock. Every night, she climbs into her woolen sleeping bag and lies down by the warm fire. She sleeps peacefully. The grown-ups chat and laugh, never worrying about waking anyone. They stir their fires and push the logs together several times during the night to keep them burning. Even in the jungle, the night air gets chilly.

The next day, Pilipinto makes friends with two young Waorani: a boy and a girl, Taementa and Bai. As they play together, Pilipinto learns to speak their language. It is nasal sounding and full of descriptive noises! Gikari wonders how Pilipinto picks up the sounds so quickly. Gikari spends days listening, asking the Waorani what words they use for everything. She writes down the sounds in a special code called phonetics. She uses a tape recorder and presses record, stop, play, and rewind over and over again, making sure she writes down exactly what they are saying.

The Waorani have never written down their language, so they have no books to read. They have never heard of the Bible. Gikari plans to tell them

the stories about God and his Son, Jesus. She works very hard for a long time to learn to speak to them.

When Pilipinto comes to tell her something, Gikari asks her to say it in Waorani as well as English. Then she tries to repeat whatever Pilipinto says. But whenever mama tries to pronounce something, Pilipinto says, "Ha aacahn!" which means, "Listen to how she says *that*!" and everyone giggles till their bellies hurt.

Do you know how Gikari and Pilipinto get food in Tiwaenu? There are no stores in the jungle and no airstrip for the missionary plane to land on. It would take days to walk to Shell Mera. Because of this, the Waorani offer Gikari some fish, or plantains to cook. Sometimes they bring them huge, delicious, wild grapes. The men hunt every day. They come home with wild boars, monkeys, or small birds that they cook and share. But Gikari cannot always depend on their kindness because they don't always kill a big animal. So the missionary plane flies over Tiwaenu and drops a bundle by parachute!

Every week when the villagers hear the hum of the little plane way off in the distance, they call out, "The yellow bumblebee is coming!" One man, Gikita, loves to guess exactly where the plane will drop its bundle. As the hum of the plane gets louder and louder, the speck grows larger and larger—until finally they can see its yellow color. Suddenly the noise is deafening as it zooms right overhead!

The pilot aims to drop the bundle right into the center of the clearing. But sometimes it lands in the forest and its parachute gets caught in a tree. Then the Indians run as fast as they can to be the first to climb the tree, grab the bundle, and untangle the ropes from the branches.

Everyone gets excited when Gikari opens the basket! There are some letters, a news magazine, oatmeal, maybe a piece of meat, instant coffee, rice, and powdered milk. These goodies are sent by the missionaries in Shell Mera. Once a month, they receive the *National Geographic* magazine! The Waorani, excited about the pictures, ask Gikari to explain what they are. After she tells them, they turn to one another and repeat exactly what she just said.

As Gikari works on writing down the Waorani language, she begins to speak it. She tells the Indians about God and his Son Jesus. Gikari, Rachel Saint (sister of Nate Saint), and Dayuma (a Waorani woman) tell the stories of the Bible. They take turns holding the Sunday morning "service."

During the service, the Indians do not sit still and listen. Instead, they nip lice out of each other's hair, slap biting bugs, and pick out the splinters in their feet. They like to keep busy while they're listening. The children have fun running back and forth to the river. Yet when they hear the stories about Jesus, the people simply believe. They never argue with, or question, the missionaries. How amazing that God prepared their hearts to hear the Truth and believe it. They are no longer violent Indians but truly Waorani—"the people" of God. This is just what Pilipinto's father had prayed for so many years before!

March, 1961

The other day Val got down the oil painting of Jim, and lay in the hammock looking at it, singing this song:

"I love you daddy, I love you, I love you. I wish you were alive. I wish you were down here. I am six years old now, I am getting big. We live in Tiwaeno, Dayuma and Auntie Rachel Live here too.

I love you, Daddy, I love you. I wish you were down here. I wish you were alive. I don't cry, though, because I don't think about you very much—I usually think about play. Dayuma is making clothes for the Waorani. Amen."

Chapter 6

A Happy Birthday

It's February 27—Pilipinto's fourth birthday! Mama has planned a birthday party. Her birthday cake arrives in the mail with a can of sticky frosting. A few stray ants find their way into the can, but the Waorani don't mind that one bit! They eagerly taste the cake, but it is too sweet for them. They decide they don't like it!

Still they are excited about their first birthday party. Gikari helps them sing "Happy Birthday." Taementa, Bai, and the other children play with balloons. They learn to play ring-around-the-rosy and Blind Man's Bluff. Pilipinto even gets to open gifts from America. Her Grandmother Elliot has sent a bright turquoise dress with silver rick-rack that she had made. What a thrill to put on a new dress after wearing sun suits most of the time! The rest of the Indians watch all of this and laugh.

The Waorani do not wear clothing—just a string around their waists. When Gikari asks why they wear the string, they exclaim, "You don't expect us to walk around naked, do you?!" No one ever told them to wear clothes, so they are perfectly content not to have any. The weather is pleasant all year long, and clothing makes them too hot. But Dayuma tells them the story of Adam and Eve, how God covered their nakedness. She promises to make clothing for them using her sewing machine, back in Shandia.

Even though Pilipinto has her own doll—and some books and crayons—she would much rather play with her Waorani friends. They can play with sticks, go swimming in the river, and catch bugs for fun. They even have pet monkeys riding on their heads! They like hacking at stumps and logs with small knives, and they gather sticks and twigs to build fires. It's easy to light their fires by taking a burning stick from one of the grown-up fires to light theirs. They even know how to keep a small fire burning in the rain.

Pilipinto teaches them how to play "house" and orders them around. She explains that she is the mama and they are the children or the daddy. She sweeps out their "house" with a feather fan, just like the real mothers do. The fan is made

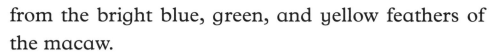

from the bright blue, green, and yellow feathers of the macaw.

Taementa and Bai teach Pilipinto to use her hands to catch small armored catfish, that cling to rocks with their mouths. Afterward, they squeeze out the guts, wrap them in leaves, roast them in the fire, and eat them. She loves doing that! They also have lots of fun catching very small crawfish. The crawfish shoot backward in the water and hide between the rocks. The children guess which way they'll go and get their hands ready to capture them. They roast, peel, and eat them too. The Waorani also eat termites, or flying ants. Since the ants come out of the ground at night, they use a flaming torch to find them. The termites are about two inches long, with red, velvety bodies and thin gossamer wings. After they roast them in hot ashes, the Indians show Pilipinto how to pull off the wings. Then she pops the whole ant body into her mouth. It tastes like bacon!

On most days, Gikari cooks rice and fried eggs. Even though this is Pilipinto's favorite meal, she asks, "Can I watch the others eat?" She knows it is not polite to ask the Indians for food. But when she goes over to watch

them, they always give her their monkey or fish. They teach her how to suck the marrow out of the bones, the brains out of the monkey's skull, and the eyeballs out of the fish heads! When the Wao eat, they do not talk but concentrate on eating. All you hear is sucking and slurping! There is nothing left of any creature they eat except bones.

One day, Gikari and Pilipinto visit missionaries in Quito. When fish is served for dinner, Pilipinto is disappointed. Not wanting to be rude, she whispers to her mama, "Where's the head?" and Gikari smiles and says, "You may go in the kitchen and ask if you may have it." When the meal is finished, Pilipinto follows the hostess to the kitchen and asks if she can have the fish's head. But unfortunately, the hostess has already thrown it away!

Gikari does not need to entertain her little girl, because she can bathe in the river, pull weeds, cut papaya stalks for toy blowguns, tend to her can of tadpoles, or follow the men on a fishing trip. She loves going into the jungle to find wild grapes or to suck drops of nectar from flower blossoms.

The Waorani often catch baby birds and nurse them to adulthood. Pilipinto has endless hours of fun taking care of them.

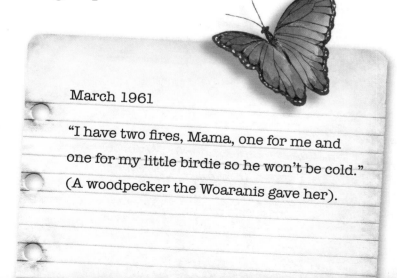

March 1961

"I have two fires, Mama, one for me and one for my little birdie so he won't be cold." (A woodpecker the Woaranis gave her).

The older boys capture a big bumblebee. They tie a piece of string with a wad of cotton-like kapok to it. Then they watch it fly round and round until it is too tired to fly anymore. When it lands, they laugh at the poor thing.

When the Waorani children slip or fall into a mud puddle, their parents do not seem to care, so their children have no time to feel sorry for themselves. They all (even Pilipinto) learn to laugh at many little hurts and bruises.

The children tease one another as all children do around the world. Even adults will kid them with horrifying stories of their mothers leaving them or roasting them in a fire. One of the men, named Dabu, tells Pilipinto he is going to chop her up with an ax! She runs away shrieking, but Mama tells her that he didn't mean it! As the Waorani understand the teaching to love one another, they learn to be more loving.

When Pilipinto grows up, she will tell her children, "Don't tease your brother or sister, even if you are only kidding! It is not kind to tease."

Chapter 7

Kept Safe

It's nighttime in the rainforest, and Pilipinto is sleeping peacefully. Gikari looks down at her daughter. Is the roof leaking? There seems to be a puddle on her bed. When she reaches down to touch the puddle, it turns out to be a black snake coiled up on Pilipinto's sleeping bag! It darts off the bed and slithers back into the jungle. Gikari thanks God for protecting them both from being bitten. They are learning that God and his angels are watching over them. He will keep them safe.

Any place where Pilipinto can lie down near a warm fire is home. Her Mama always sings hymns to her as she falls asleep. Her two favorites are "Jesus, Tender Shepherd, Hear Me" and "The Lord's My Shepherd, I'll Not Want." Do you know these hymns? You should look them up and sing them too!

Sometimes Pilipinto sings with her mama, and after her prayers, she makes up her own songs. She even makes up a song to sing to her daddy. She cannot remember him because he died when she was so small, but she knows he is up in heaven.

During her prayers, she asks, "God, why did you make jellyfish and tigers?" She has seen both tigers and jellyfish in the *National Geographic* magazine. There are no tigers in the Amazon jungles. But there are jaguars, pumas, panthers, and large cats called ocelots that look like miniature leopards. Big cats like to hunt for small animals like chickens. That can be a problem for the Waorani!

One night, a few of the Waorani's chickens mysteriously disappear. In the morning, the men discuss what to do about it. Pilipinto watches while they build a trap to catch the animal that is stealing their chickens. The trap is made out of smooth, straight sticks tied with palm fronds. It has a door that slams shut after the animal goes in to catch a chicken.

The next night, Gikita wakes the missionaries. He motions for them to come and see something. As they walk across the clearing through a soft rain, they hear an animal snarling and growling. The ocelot's eyes glow as they shine a flashlight in its face. It pokes its paws out of the trap, angrily scratching and clawing at the wood. Pilipinto is glad that it can't get out of the cleverly made trap. Now she feels safe going back to bed. In the morning she sees its skin stretched out to dry between two poles. Pilipinto keeps the skin to show to her own children some day!

To survive in the rainforest, the Indians must know how to hunt for food. Learning to hit an animal in just the right spot begins when children are very young. Boys practice stabbing insects with thin straws or sticks. Sometimes they kill a small brightly colored bird and pluck out all the feathers. They learn to roast it in the fire and eat the tiny bits of meat on the bones. When they grow up, they will throw spears at fish or wild boars for their families to eat.

The real spears that the men use are made of hard black wood that is carefully carved to a point on one end. The tips have notches on each side to keep the spear from being pulled back out. They kill monkeys with tiny thin darts that have poison on the end. Small darts have no notch, so the Indians can pull them back out and use them again. The darts are blown out of "blow guns." The men craft them from strong palm wood fiber. They carry quivers full of darts on their backs. All the children wear a string around their waists. The older boys hunt for birds and hang them on their strings to carry them home.

Gikita is one of the men who killed Pilipinto's father and the four other missionaries. The Waorani men speared people whom they thought were invading their territory. But when they hear that God says in his "carvings" (the Bible) not to kill, they believe in him. They tell Gikari that they will no longer kill people. And they don't! Of all the Waorani, Gikita is the most friendly and helpful to Gikari. She and Pilipinto are kept safe because God is taking care of them. He changed the hearts of the Waorani and turned the entire tribe into a loving people.

Jan. 5, 1960—evening prayer

"Thank you that we have strong legs and strong arms and two little hands to help Jesus in his work . . . "And help the Wao to love you and help everybody in the world to love you, and thank you for mommie and that sometimes I can sleep in the same bed with my mommie."

Chapter 8

Jungle School

When Pilipinto turns five, Gikari starts to teach her how to read and write. Her friends like to watch her draw pictures and write her letters. Pilipinto shows them how to paint their toes and hands with her watercolor paints. Since Pilipinto would much rather play with her friends, Gikari decides to build a house with walls. The walls will give privacy and quiet, and allow Pilipinto to finish her lessons each day.

Gikari hires some Quichua Indians to build a new bamboo house. It has strong palm wood stilts, a thatched roof, real screen windows, and a wooden floor. It even has a tiny kitchen with a wood stove, stacked boxes for cupboards, and a small counter for mama's dishpan. There are two bedrooms and a living room.

Pilipinto sits by the window that overlooks the river. She is trying to work on her lessons, but she can see and hear the children playing and splashing in the river. She can't wait to finish her schoolwork. Then she can run down to the river and play with them!

Sometimes Taementa comes to the door. He whines to be let in. Gikari insists that he learn to ask politely, "Please let me come in." But instead, he stands on the top step and whimpers for at least five minutes.

One day Pilipinto and Taementa decide to roast a grasshopper! Since they already roasted a crawfish, they think it will taste just as delicious. Still, Taementa makes Pilipinto try it first. It tastes awful! Taementa is pleased that he escaped eating it!

Even though Pilipinto has shown bravery by eating a grasshopper, she refuses to eat fat, white palm grubs. Palm grubs live in the heart of the palm tree, so they are very clean. Because the Indians have no other fat in their diet, they think grubs are a delicacy! Why does she try a grasshopper, but turn her nose up at a grub worm?

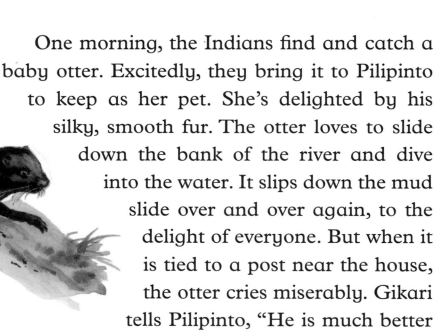

One morning, the Indians find and catch a baby otter. Excitedly, they bring it to Pilipinto to keep as her pet. She's delighted by his silky, smooth fur. The otter loves to slide down the bank of the river and dive into the water. It slips down the mud slide over and over again, to the delight of everyone. But when it is tied to a post near the house, the otter cries miserably. Gikari tells Pilipinto, "He is much better off on his own in the wild. That's where he'll be happiest."

That afternoon, when Pilipinto finishes her schoolwork, they watch the otter slide down the bank one last time. She waves goodbye as he swims down the river. The Waorani tenderly take care of their pets. But they know when it is time to let them fend for themselves in the jungle.

In the hot afternoon, Pilipinto goes with the Indian women to work in their manioc gardens. She keeps busy swatting mosquitoes as sweat trickles down her face. The manioc root is like a potato that the Indians peel and then boil in a pot. After it is cooked, they eat the boiled chunks or make chicha out of it. Chicha is made in a very strange way. The women chew

the manioc first, then spit it out into a wooden tray. They wrap it up like a package in a banana leaf and leave it alone for a couple of days. When they unwrap it, they put it in a gourd and mix it with water. It is sour and stringy, but Pilipinto loves it. Sometimes it is all that the men and women eat before going on a full day's journey.

The Indians teach Pilipinto and Gikari to live life day by day. When the jungle is rainy and miserable, with hundreds of biting insects, the Waorani accept this as part of life. They do not whine or complain. Often they don't have much food to eat, because the men can't kill a large animal every day. But even with just one small meal a day, they don't grumble.

Pilipinto learns to like foods that most little girls in the world don't eat. Since the Waorani live off the land, she eats many delicious fruits that can't be bought or grown anywhere else! When the Indians offer to do things for her and Gikari, she learns to be kind and helpful. The Wao weave hammocks and chigras (woven net bags), make clay pots, and bring fish they have speared in the river to the missionaries.

The Waorani love to laugh! They find excitement in the simplest pleasures— like swimming, walking, and watching the animals or birds. This gives Pilipinto her love of God's creation. Growing up in the jungle teaches her to enjoy what God has given.

Gikari watches the Indians accept their simple life in the rainforest. She wonders why people who live with TV, radios, phones, cars, and stores are so anxious to have *more things*. But *things* don't bring them true happiness. God's Word says, "If we have food and clothing, we will be content with that" (1 Timothy 6:8 NIV). God is pleased with us when we are thankful even in hard times. Gikari and Pilipinto love their simple life in Tiwaenu. They would like to stay with their Waorani friends forever. But God has planned more work for them to do back in Shandia.

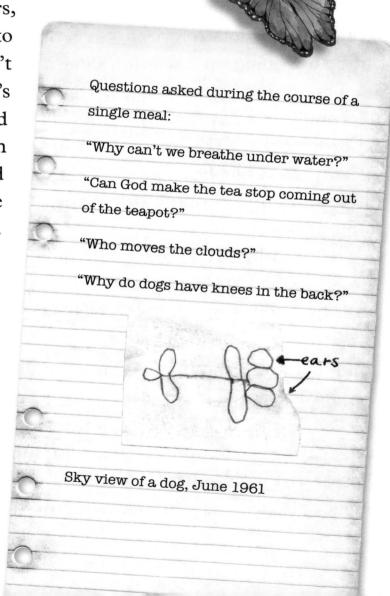

Questions asked during the course of a single meal:

"Why can't we breathe under water?"

"Can God make the tea stop coming out of the teapot?"

"Who moves the clouds?"

"Why do dogs have knees in the back?"

ears

Sky view of a dog, June 1961

Chapter 9

Home to Shandia

"*Señora Mama* is home!" The Quichuas run and greet Gikari with hugs! It has been two years since Mama and Pilipinto left for Tiwaenu. Now Señora has come back to Shandia to teach and translate more of the Bible into Quichua.

Pilipinto and Mama move into the Elliots' house that Jim built before he was killed. Pilipinto is just as happy here as she was in Tiwaenu. This "new" home is very big and exciting to her. She has her own room with a small wooden bed that her daddy had built for her. It has a pretty pink and white-striped skirt around it. She loves to snuggle under the clean white sheet and warm blanket. It feels cozy when the rain pours down outside and drums on the tin roof. Because there is no glass in the windows, the rain is very loud. It splashes on the gravel around the house and on the banana tree leaves.

A Quichua Indian woman lives upstairs with her daughter, Alicia. The mother helps Señora Mama with cooking and housework. Pilipinto plays house too. Using her own miniature wicker table and chairs, she hosts tea

parties for Alicia and their dolls. Sometimes they ask permission to walk a little way through the rainforest to play with the other children.

Pilipinto and her mama live close to a huge rushing river. Pilipinto patiently pans for gold with the other children, but they never find any. Sometimes she ventures into the forest where there is a huge rock over a deep pool. Together, they love jumping into the pool by leaping off the rock!

Once Pilipinto's mama let her stay overnight at a friend's house. She had to sleep on a low split-bamboo bed with rolled-up clothes for a pillow. This flat pillow was harder than her soft pillow at home and the bamboo slats pinched her! Pilipinto woke up to the sound of her friend's mother stirring the soup. As she stirred, she steadily blew on the coals to keep the soup cooking. Pilipinto was glad to get up from the pinching bamboo bed and squat by the fire. When her friend woke up, they each got a white metal bowl of soup. It tasted good!

When she got home, Mama asked her what she had for breakfast. "Soup," Pilipinto said matter-of-factly.

Mama asked, "What kind?"

"Rat," said Pilipinto.

The huge jungle rats eat plants, not garbage, so they are "clean" compared to the rats in the cities.

Pilipinto and Mama share an office, a small room with two desks and a blackboard. Pilipinto has her own desk where she does her schoolwork. Mama types letters at her desk and keeps working on translations. The word *THIMK!* is on the blackboard. It is spelled wrong to remind Pilipinto to think hard about her spelling and her arithmetic.

Pilipinto has a hard time concentrating on her schoolwork. She wants to be outside playing. Often her friends sneak up to the window, and if Mama is not there, they loudly whisper, "Pilipinto, shami!" But she isn't allowed to go out and play until all her schoolwork is done.

June 1961—School picnic:

We went a long, long ways and then we found a little lake. We couldn't find any rocks to sit on so we found a little stream and then we sat down on leaves and ate. And we got some water and made some lemonade. Then we drank it. Then we ate our food—sandwich and carrots and peanuts, and then we ate our dessert. That was candy and chocolate and marshmallow. We went home on the trail, then we went in the water and then we came home.

In the end, Pilipinto's mama teaches her to love reading. When Pilipinto grows up and becomes a mother, she loves reading out loud to her children. She also makes them do their schoolwork before they can go outside and play!

Chapter 10

Lessons of Life and Death

Before Pilipinto's daddy was killed, he had started many projects to help the Indians. Now Señora supervises all the work that must be done and teaches men and women how to read the Bible and sing hymns. While Mama works, Pilipinto plays outside. She happily runs about in the front yard in sunshine or in pouring rain. If it is sunny, she chases brilliantly colored butterflies, which, as you know, is why the Indians call her Pilipinto!

After a hard rain one day, a giant earthworm appears on the front porch. They look exactly like the ones you have seen—except they are two to three feet longer! Pilipinto bends down to study one as it inches along. She is thankful she doesn't have to pick it up! Why did God make some creatures beautiful and others ugly?

One day while they're eating in the dining room, they hear the teacups rattling in their saucers! The ground rumbles as it shakes under their feet! Almost as soon as it starts, the shaking stops. Pilipinto is startled! "What happened?" she asks Mama.

"That was an earthquake!" Mama tells her. "But we are always in God's care."

The Indians are curious and like to watch Señora, Pilipinto, and their guests eat their meals. They peek through the screen windows and wait for Señora to answer their questions. When the foreigners bow their heads to pray, the Indians whisper to each other, "Atsai, atsai, atsai!" That means they are embarrassed and don't know what to do or where to look. Sometimes their Quichua friends ask for help. Señora may need to give them a shot of medicine or buy a chicken from them.

Every day, God's angels are watching over Pilipinto. Today, her mama asks her to take a note to Venancio. It means she will have to walk down the path of bamboo logs, through the jungle, to the clearing for the airstrip—all by herself! To keep from getting scared, she sings to herself as she walks.

While trotting home, she sees a snake up ahead, waiting on the side of the trail. It is poised to strike toward the center of the path! What should she do? Turn back and run?

No—Pilipinto walks quickly but quietly past the snake. Her heart beats fast, but the snake does not strike. As soon as she is far enough away, she runs as fast as her legs can carry her. She races across the stream and up the hill to her house. She slams the screen door behind her as she runs inside.

"Mama!" she cries. "I saw a snake on the path!"

"Oh?" Mama says calmly as she keeps working at the stove.

Pilipinto feels a little embarrassed that she is so scared. Her mama doesn't seem to be a bit anxious. God makes her fearless as she entrusts her little girl into his loving hands.

Thankfully, not all the animals in the jungle are dangerous. Pilipinto's small pet monkey, "Boogie," lives in a tree outside their kitchen. He has his own little house to sleep in. A rope around his neck ties him to the tree to keep him from running away. It is long enough so that he can climb down to the ground and run around. Pilipinto loves watching him. She giggles seeing him hold a butterfly or a beetle in his hands. He chatters to himself as he turns it over and over before popping it into his mouth.

Boogie is her favorite pet! She cries when they discover her beloved monkey is very sick. When he dies, Pilipinto learns that this is part of life.

Señora Mama is often called to help save the lives of Indian mothers in childbirth. She takes Pilipinto along with her. One baby needs to be wrapped in a cloth immediately. The other women who want to help are so sure the baby will die that they refuse to get the cloth. Mama asks Pilipinto to go and fetch it for her. Pilipinto obeys quickly. She runs to get it, and the child's life is saved!

But sadly, Señora cannot save everyone. On another day she and Pilipinto are called to treat a sick child. When they arrive, the child is already dead. The whole family cries the death wail and covers the child with a blanket. Pilipinto knows that death is a fearful thing. But she also knows that because Jesus rose from the dead, she can trust him to take her to heaven when she dies.

Knowing her daddy is in heaven gives Pilipinto confidence that she can live for God and trust him to take care of her. She looks forward to seeing her daddy one day. She often dreams that he has come back to be with them and they are singing and laughing together. Mama says, "Your daddy had a strong voice that could sing very loudly. He wrote thoughts in his journal like 'Live life to the hilt' and 'Wherever you are, be all there!' That means that God wants you to work and play with all your heart."

Just like her daddy, Pilipinto loves being in the jungle! And, like her daddy, she learns how to work hard and glorify God with her whole heart.

Perhaps God put you in a small country town, or a city, or a suburb, and maybe your house is very small, like Pilipinto's house in Tiwaenu. Yet whatever size your house is, and whatever the land looks like outside, if you believe in Jesus Christ, he will always guide you and help you. He will take care of you just as perfectly as he took care of Pilipinto. He will be with you and love you more than you know.

Friends forever . . .

"I thought I would never see you till we got to heaven!"

Once as a grownup, Pilipinto traveled to Ecuador to visit the Quichua Indians. One of her girlfriends from Shandia met her "by accident" while they were riding together on a crowded bus. When they recognized each other, tears welled up in their eyes. The Indian friend said, "I thought I would never see you till we got to heaven!" She was one of the little girls that had played in Pilipinto's playhouse.

Books and Films

- Elisabeth Elliot Foundation Library of Books: elisabethelliot.org
- End of the Spear film: www.christiancinema.com/digital/movie/end-of-the-spear
- Follow Valerie Elliot Shepard on Facebook and Instagram (Velliotofficial)

Pronunciation Guide

Pilipinto (pee-lee-PEEN-toh)
Quichua (KEE-chuah)
Quito (KEE-toh)
Shandia (SHAN-dee-uh)
Shell Mera (shell-MEH-rah)
Waorani (wah-oh-DAH-nee)
Wao (Wow)
Tiwaenu (tee-WAH-noo)
"ha aacahn!" (HAH-ah-KAH)
"atsai" (aht-SIGH)
"shami" (SHAH-mee)

chigras (CHEE-grahs)
chicha (CHEE-chuh)
Gikari (gee-KAH-ree)
Mintaka (min-TAH-kuh)
Mankamu (man-KAH-moo)
Fermin (FEHR-min)
Venancio (veh-NAHN-see-oh)
Taementa (tie-MEN-tuh)
Bai (BYE)
Dayuma (die-YOO-muh)
Gikita (gee-KEE-tuh)

To hear Valerie Shepard pronounce these Quichua and Waorani words, scan the QR code or go to www.prpbooks.com/book/pilipinto

61

About the Author

Valerie Elliot Shepard was born in Ecuador in 1955, and spent her early years living in the Amazon Jungle with the Quichua Indians and the Waorani Indians. She is the only daughter of Jim and Elisabeth Elliot, missionaries to Ecuador.

Valerie returned to the United States in 1963 to live in New Hampshire. After graduating from Wheaton College in 1976, she married Walter Shepard, a Presbyterian minister who is now retired. The Lord gave them eight children whom they homeschooled, and eleven grandchildren.

Valerie speaks at women's events and continues to write. She has written three books—*Devotedly*, the love story of her parents—*Pilipinto*, the exciting story of her life in Ecuador—and *If*, co-authored with Jim Palumbo, a devotional by Amy Carmichael. She and Walt both lead active lives of Christian ministry and currently reside in Long Beach, Mississippi.

About the Artist

Jim Howard (Valerie's uncle) began drawing at an early age. After studying at the American Academy of Art in Chicago, he worked as a freelance artist and illustrated books for various publishers. He works in watercolor, pen and ink, and pencil. Jim has pastored churches in Minnesota, Wyoming, and Montana. He and his late wife, Joyce, have four grown children, and he lives in Bozeman, Montana. To see his work, visit www.jnhoward-watercolor.com.